The Mindset Method

*How to Get Out Of Your Own Way
in Life & Business*

Jaime Ellithorpe

Table of Contents

Introduction 9

My Mindset Journey 13

Understanding Limiting Beliefs 17

The Courage to Work on Yourself 21

The Process of Having it All 23

Recognizing Your Thoughts 25

What's Next? 31

How to Get What You Want 33

Eat the Elephant 37

Roadblocks When You're Manifesting 43

You Already Have What it Takes 49

Perfection Versus Perfect Harmony 51

When You Don't Do the Work 55

What I Wish I'd Known Sooner 65

Action Steps 69

Now's the Time 73

Introduction

Many business owners get so caught up in the tactical aspects of their business. They're either looking for the silver bullet to grow their business, or they're looking for some magical strategy to get quick results.

While there are some great strategies out there to grow a business, what a lot of business owners don't realize is that they are preventing their own success. It's because they don't have a clear mindset that's aligned to reach the goals they're looking to reach. Mindset is huge.

When you have the right mindset, the dreams and goals you aspire to and everything you have ever envisioned for your business start coming together easily and effortlessly. As your goals and dreams start to manifest, it just feels like breathing. It feels like the natural next step because you've aligned your thoughts and energy to match the equivalent of the physical creation.

Most people think fireworks will go off once they finally achieve their goals, but it won't be like that at all. Because the idea of having what they want feels so far away, they think it will feel like a huge accomplishment once they achieve it. The feeling of your goals being so far away is actually an indicator that your mindset is full of beliefs that are preventing you from achieving your goals and dreams.

When achieving your goals starts to feel effortless, that is when you know that you have cleared your mindset enough and done enough mental strength training to reach them. The most important thing you can do for yourself and your business is get into the mindset of expectation and knowing what you want is on its way to becoming reality.

As humans, it's our tendency to doubt. When we question ourselves and our abilities, that's what stops us from reaching our dreams and our goals. Instead, feel empowered by what you've overcome and achieved already in life, and realize that your past is simply a stepping stone that's moving you in the right direction towards manifesting your goals and dreams!

My Mindset Journey

My journey started back in corporate America. I did essentially what society said I should do. I went to college. I got a degree. I moved to one of the largest cities in the United States, Dallas, Texas. I was a small-town girl from Southwest Iowa, so it was a big step for me to come to Dallas.

I got a job that ended up putting me in the corporate space, and I did very well in that job. I ended up moving out of that job and landed a really good job at the largest company within the industry; a job that many internal employees had fought for.

Once I got that job, I realized I had been on this path of building, trying to keep moving forward, thinking I was going to be really happy when I achieved my job goals. Unfortunately, when I got there, I felt empty and knew there had to be more to life.

That's how I started down the path of my own mindset journey. I just had this feeling that there was something more, but I just couldn't quite put my finger on it. I was determined to figure it all out.

Around this time a friend invited me to a bookstore. He was looking for something specific in one of the sections of the store, so I was left to my own devices.

I happened to walk up to an end cap with several featured books, and one of them practically jumped off the shelf. The cover was interesting, so I picked it up. I flipped the book over, and the back cover said that I had the power to create whatever I wanted in my life. I just needed to know a few things in order to do that.

The concept intrigued me, so I bought the book. The book was about the law of attraction and the basics of using your mind to create whatever you want in life and business by aligning your thoughts with your goals and dreams.

I devoured the entire book in just a few days, and after that, I just went on this full-on journey of studying everything I could about mindset and how the universal law of attraction works in our everyday lives.

Essentially, I learned that the barriers we have hidden in our mindset at a subconscious level are what stop all of us. These are not the same as the thoughts we know we are thinking. These are the thoughts going on in the background that we are not aware of, and they sabotage us and make us feel like we are never going to reach our goals.

Over time I collaborated all of the information I studied from many different people—law of attraction practitioners, spiritual leaders, physicists, biologists, psychiatrists, mindset experts, and many others—and developed my own protocol to work on my mindset.

Fast forward to today, and it has been through a series of working on myself and doing a lot of mental strength training exercises that I've been able to clear my mind of so many things that held me back in my own business.

I've now achieved and am still achieving the dreams and goals that I set when I was a child. It is all now coming to reality, and it's amazing to think back to all of this feeling impossible just a few years ago!

Understanding Limiting Beliefs

Most people have what are called limiting beliefs. These are beliefs hidden in the subconscious mind, and they create an invisible barrier to getting what you want. Two of the most common limiting beliefs are: "I don't deserve it" and "I'm not good enough."

When we start to dig down the rabbit hole of all of these different layers of excuses and barriers that are really stopping us—whether that's fear, doubt, worry, or overwhelm—at the root of all those feelings are typically these two limiting beliefs.

I think as a business owner, these two beliefs are important to look at because if you don't feel like you deserve to have the business that you really want, or you don't feel like you deserve to have the success that you know is in your heart, then you will self-sabotage.

This is what I was talking about earlier when I said that you can have all the best strategies in the world implemented in your business, but if you don't feel like you deserve the business success, then you'll self-sabotage all of those strategies that you've got going on in your business. Most people blame the tools and strategies and never even think about how they might be subconsciously self-sabotaging their own success.

The other common limiting belief, feeling like you're not good enough to have something, is something I think we pick up in our early years from society.

Being told 'no' by your mom, your dad, your teacher, or a caregiver is what can set the stage for that kind of limiting belief, and we go about our lives picking up more experiences that just further feed the 'not good enough' limiting belief.

By the time we're adults and we decide to start a business, we've got those hidden beliefs anchored in the back of our minds at a subconscious level. It's these hidden beliefs that are preventing business growth and client acquisition, not marketing or sales strategies.

I addressed these limiting beliefs in my own journey, and once I did, that had the most profound impact on the growth and success of my business. The marketing and sales strategies I had in place started working like clockwork, and clients started coming out of the woodwork. As an added benefit, other areas of my life started to improve as well!

The Courage to Work on Yourself

Many people realize they are blocking themselves from getting what they want in life and in business, but many of them are afraid to unlock Pandora's Box and take a look inside their minds. They're afraid of what they might find, and they're scared that if they find something that they don't like, they may not be able to fix it.

The good news is opening that box is not nearly as scary as you might think. It's actually empowering to realize that you can have the tools and resources at your fingertips to remove the blocks, the barriers, and the chains that have been holding you back for so long.

You really can get everything that you've ever wanted! All you need are just a few tools and a little bit of knowledge on how to implement them to really get the freedom that you've been craving for so long. Just have the courage to take this next step. You won't be sorry you did!

The Process of Having it All

The first step in this process of having what you want is awareness. That means simply becoming aware of the thoughts and feelings that you have. Many people run on what I'll call 'programming' or unconscious thought, and they don't even stop to think about what's playing in their head or what's making them feel bad.

Day in and day out, most people run on a thought loop. They have the same series of thoughts over and over again, and it's this series of thoughts that through repetition become embedded in their subconscious mind. Once they're embedded, they form the energetic pattern for everything that manifests into reality.

If you have the 'I don't deserve it' belief, for example, you might not be able to reach your business goals, you might have an unhappy relationship with your partner, or you might be out of shape. It's the core beliefs that create your reality in every area of your life and business.

Now that you understand limiting beliefs and know you should become aware of the thousands of thoughts you have each day, you're probably wondering how you start to find the thoughts that might be sabotaging what you really want in life and business. Let's talk about that next.

Recognizing Your Thoughts

The first step to successfully recognizing your thoughts is to set the intention to notice what you're thinking. Some people may need to take time out of their day and go to a quiet place where they can sit and let their minds run, writing down the things that come up for them.

Others may not need to take time out of their day; they can just keep a journal next to them and occasionally write down thoughts. If you want to try the journal method, you can set a timer to go off several times a day, and when the timer goes off, write down what you've just been thinking. Do whatever works for you, but this first step of recording your thoughts is crucial in order for the next steps in this process to be successful.

Once you've got your thoughts down on paper, the second step is to start looking at each of your thoughts and see what patterns exist.

I suggest you record your thoughts for at least a few days so that you can start seeing your thought patterns. We tend to run on mental programs, which are essentially repeated patterns of thought looping in the back of our minds. Once you're aware of your patterns, the next thing you can do is start to recognize how those thoughts make you feel.

In the simplest of terms, when you think a thought and it does not feel good to you, then that's an indicator the thought is not in alignment with where you want to go. When you do feel good after having a thought, then that's an indicator that you're on point to achieve whatever goal or dream you have in mind. Your feelings are the temperature check.

As you're becoming aware of your thoughts, you want to start seeing how they line up with what it is you want. If you have thoughts that don't line up, that's when you can take the next step to shift and align them with where you want to go.

A lot of people get trapped in self-judgment when they start to recognize their thoughts. They say, "Oh my gosh, I can't believe that I think this, I'm embarrassed," or "Shame on me, how dare I think something like that!" A sea of emotions starts coming out. In this process, it's not about labeling any of these thoughts or emotions; it's about recognizing them, so you know whether you are on track or not with your goals and dreams. It's all about energetic alignment.

With that in mind, the third step in this process is to objectively look at your thoughts and feelings. The more that you can step outside of yourself and become a third-party observer, the better you're going to be at recognizing your thoughts.

It would almost be like if your best friend disclosed to you everything that was going on in his or her head. You wouldn't really have an emotional reaction to it, right? You would just be able to observe the thoughts and say, "Oh, that's interesting," or "You know that's a new way to look at that..." That's how you want to act with your own mindset. You're simply looking and observing. Realize you really just want to go down the rabbit hole in your mind to see what is there.

Speaking of going down the rabbit hole, are you sure your thoughts are even really yours? If most of your thoughts are simply programming that's been installed in your brain from society your whole life, how do you know what you really think? If it helps to remove yourself from the situation and pretend these thoughts really aren't yours, then take that approach.

The more that you can distance yourself from your thoughts and step back, the easier it is to address the things that are stopping you. Keep reminding yourself that your thoughts are outside of who you really are; you are not your thoughts.

The goal of this entire process is to remove all of the layers of limiting beliefs and feelings that don't feel good, so that you are living authentically and you're able to line up who you really are with your business.

When you do those things, you are absolutely on fire! You'll achieve everything you've ever wanted and more. You'll help all the people who you've always wanted to help through your business and make a big difference in the world.

What's Next?

Another mindset trap that many people fall into is they're really clear on what they don't want but not clear on what they do want. You'll recognize these people as the gripers and the complainers, who unfortunately make up a huge part of society.

 The reason they complain is because that's their comfort zone. What they're complaining about is their current reality, so it seems logical to complain. What they don't realize is that their complaining and focusing on what they don't want is what's actually creating their reality!

This pattern is very hard to break because the more you complain, the more you perpetuate creating that same reality, and the more that this reality is sitting in front of you, the easier it is to complain. So, what do you do?

The good news is you can leverage knowing what you don't like or don't want to manifest what you do want. We live on a planet of duality, meaning every topic on earth also has its opposite. Think black and white. Up and down. Left and right.

Because you're clear on what you don't want, you can go to the opposite side of the spectrum to get clear on what you do want. We'll talk about how to take what you don't want and use it as fuel to power what you do want in the next section.

How to Get What You Want

It's now time to get clear on what you want! A great exercise to help you get clear is to fold a piece of paper in half, and on one side write down everything that you don't want.

Unfold the paper (and draw a line down the middle if you want). Look at each thing you wrote down that you don't want, and then think about what you do want or how you'd like things to be instead. Write down whatever you want on the same line but the opposite half of the paper.

Once you're clear on what you want, you may start to doubt or fear you can't have it. This is the mindset work. It's the everyday training of clearing your mind of doubt, worry, and fear and bringing in the good feeling emotions that match the feeling of accomplishing your goals and dreams.

Aligning yourself with thoughts that match what it is you do want—and feeling today how you'll feel once you have whatever it is you want—is using the law of attraction to manifest it easily and effortlessly.

The other piece of getting what you want is the process of removing the mental barriers that are preventing you from raising your energetic vibration and matching the energy of what it is that you'd like to create.

It's really a few schools of thought that I have blended together to help people get on the fast track to reaching their goals and dreams. What we do in my process is start looking at the feelings that don't feel good. In my experience coaching business owners, it's mostly fear, doubt, worry, and overwhelm that keep them stuck.

Those are the top things that I see that come up for most business owners. So, it's removing all of the layers of those four emotions while working towards creating the reality that they would really, really like to have. It's a blend of the law of attraction exercises and mindset training to start focusing your brain on what you do want while taking the focus off what you don't want.

Eat the Elephant

As they say, how do you eat an elephant? One bite at a time, right?

With that in mind, start with just one manifestation or goal to focus on. What I have clients do first is draw out the big picture of where they want to go. If you'd like to manifest a business or something in your business, where would you like your business to be one year from now?

Create an overarching clear picture of what the big goal looks like, and then inside that picture, line out some specific goals or some projects that line up to achieving the big goal. Maybe these smaller goals are to be reached every quarter or once a month, for example.

Once you have all your goals set, I suggest you pick one small goal and work on manifesting it by removing the mindset barriers that have blocked you from achieving it up until now.

Let's just use a project as an example. Maybe you want to create a course to offer your clients and you want to have it done six months from today. The first thing that's probably going to happen is there's a part of you that feels really good and excited about creating the course. There's another part of you that has some type of fear around releasing this program to the world and being judged for it, or maybe you doubt that anybody will buy it.

You might worry that it takes too much time to work on building the course and you've got other things to do in your business. People create all of these stories in their heads about how their business is going to backslide and fail because they're spending all this time working on this course, and just the thought of adding another project to their plate throws them into complete overwhelm.

Removing this inner conflict is the work. When there's a part of you that really, really wants something, but then you've got all this underlying stuff that's stopping you from taking the physical action you need to take to get it done, you must remove the invisible limiting beliefs to get results.

The way to do this is to unload all of those thoughts and feelings, layer by layer. Remember earlier when I mentioned mindset training? Mindset training is very much like peeling an onion. When you cut open an onion, you see all the layers inside. That's a lot like your mind. There are many layers of thoughts and feelings that must be uncovered and addressed in order to achieve your goals and dreams easily and effortlessly.

You might doubt that you can create a course, for example, but when you start to look at doubt, that feeling has probably mushroomed into many areas of your life. Doubt is probably not just in your business.

So, just removing doubt in general is going to not only move your business forward, but it's going to make your life better all the way around.

When you start to remove the various layers of thoughts and emotions that are not in alignment with where you want to go, you start to feel lighter. You start to get more headroom and the endless inner chatter stops. It's almost like taking off a pair of dirty glasses or removing a veil that's been shrouding your vision.

You start getting so much more clarity. Inspired ideas start to come to you to help you get this course done. Maybe someone will show up who can help create this course for you, or maybe a new client will come along who needs the exact training you'd teach in your course, so you create the content for your client and sell it later as a course. All these infinite possibilities are now open to exist once your mindset is clear.

When your mindset has been freed up to accept all possibilities, that's when things start to get really, really fun and interesting! The more that you remove the mindset barriers, the more effortless your business and life get because you're opening those channels within your mind to accept bigger, more expansive ideas.

The universe is able to bring inspired ideas to you because you won't reject them anymore. You're open to receiving something in a new way that you wouldn't have accepted previously.

Roadblocks When You're Manifesting

What should you do when you're in the process of removing mindset blocks and you come across something you don't want to face or address? The best thing to do is be honest with yourself by just saying, "I'm not here to judge myself. I'm not here to judge anyone from my past who may have helped create some of these barriers." This is not about judgment on yourself or anyone. Know that there's no blame here. There's no shame.

Mindset training is just about getting better and getting to a good place in life and in your business. Just accepting that alone is going to help you open your mind.

The way to recognize when your mind has a block goes back to recognizing that when you have a thought about where you'd like to go, it doesn't feel good. For all of us, that's our indicator that we've got something there that's preventing us from having it. Learning to be hyper-vigilant and aware of all of your thoughts is what's going to help you open your mind up the fastest.

You don't have to necessarily know what's causing the block in the beginning; it's just knowing and recognizing that there is one. I think most people recognize when there's a block, but they either avoid it completely or they push down the thought or emotion.

Avoiding the feeling is only going to bury it further and create more problems down the road. By not addressing the block, you're just creating a bigger version of this energy pattern that will have to be dealt with later. You will end up manifesting something in your physical reality that is going to eventually force you to address it.

It's kind of like that old saying, "An ounce of prevention is worth a pound of cure." The sooner you address something, the less pain you will be in later.

I personally don't like to be in a lot of pain, physically, mentally, or emotionally, so I like to address things as soon as I recognize them. That's what a lot of this work is about. If you really just want to have an easy life without much pain, then mindset training is the road to get there.

Many people will feel blocks either in their solar plexus or lower stomach area. Some may feel them in their chest, their upper back, or their head. Those tend to be places where people carry stress, so that's where a lot of our emotions are also buried. Just sitting with yourself and observing a feeling, not trying to figure it out or label it, and not judging yourself or anyone else for that feeling are some of the keys to removing blocks.

Monitoring a feeling as it moves throughout your body is one of the quickest ways to dispel it. Blocks are just stuck energy that needs to be released since we are energetic beings at our core.

We are designed to have clear energetic pathways in and around our bodies, so when energy gets stuck (in the form of thoughts and emotions), we are blocking the flow of energy.

Thoughts and feelings become stuck energy when they don't have a channel to move because for whatever reason we've prevented their release. When we open ourselves up to the possibility of just being able to release some of these thoughts and feelings, some of them will just dissipate on their own.

The key is just making sure that you're not forcing blocks to release. Mindset training is all about being in a state of allowing and not having resistance to observing and releasing blocks. It's the resistance that keeps a lot of our emotions and thoughts stuck. We resist because we want to bury thoughts and feelings that don't feel good.

Our natural instinct is, "Oh, I shouldn't think that," or "Oh, I shouldn't feel that way," and so we bury things. When you bury thoughts and feelings, that's when they get stuck, and then after enough time, they will cause emotional and physical pain.

Unfortunately, if these blocks are ignored long enough, they can even turn into disease. Many people don't look at their thoughts and emotions when they are sick because they've been conditioned to treat the outer symptoms, but when you break down the word disease into "dis-ease", it makes sense that our stuck energy would eventually manifest into a physical malady.

You Already Have What it Takes

Everything that you've ever wanted in your business and in your life comes from inside yourself and exudes out.

So many people chase their outside reality thinking that is the path to getting what they want. They say things like, "'I just need this next marketing strategy', or 'If I could just get one more client', or 'I'll be so happy when I start making this X amount of money in my business.'"

It's always this outer stuff in the future that people think is going to make them happy. What people don't realize is they are just chasing an elusive dream because they are creating their current unhappiness.

Unless they change their thoughts and feelings, they won't be able to get on the path to their desires because the desire and the current reality exist on two different energetic frequencies.

We are co-creators with the universe as it relates to the physical world, but we must understand the way the universe works in order to have the life and business we desire.

It is through our mindset that we create, and when we are free of limiting beliefs and other blocks, we've opened the energy channel so the universe can bring forth our manifestations in unlimited ways. It just requires getting out of our own way!

Perfection Versus Perfect Harmony

Perfect harmony is when you're in energetic alignment where you've cleared your mindset from all the doubt, worries, fears, overwhelm, and other limiting beliefs that have prevented you from having what you want.

The limiting thoughts and bad feeling emotions are never going to align with what it is that you want, so they must be removed. When you clear your mind of these limitations and then focus on how good it feels to have what it is you want, then you are in perfect harmony with your desire.

Perfect harmony is not about being perfect. Perfectionism is actually another mindset issue created through programming from society. Perfect harmony is about understanding that there is a formula to creating the life and business that you've always wanted and being a willing participant in using this formula to create it.

The formula for creation is a set of rules you can follow to easily and effortlessly get whatever it is that you want in your life and business. You just have to make sure that you're playing by the rules. When you don't play by the rules, life and business get hard.

Let's say, for example, your goal is to have your business do well so that you can buy that million-dollar house at the end of the street. When you drive by that house, it seems so unattainable to you—you feel like there's no way you could ever have it.

Those thoughts and feelings are the perfect indicator that you're not anywhere mentally or energetically close to being able to have the house. The work is to remove the thoughts and feelings that contradict you having the house.

You must bridge the gap from the house feeling unattainable to having the house feel as effortless as taking your next breath. You must see it happening in your mind and begin to feel how good it will feel to have the house in order to manifest it.

Once you've removed all of the mental barriers to attaining it, you can easily step into that new reality because you are free to energetically line up with the energy of the million-dollar house. All the resources you'll need to get the house will start showing up in your physical reality, and it will feel like the next natural, logical step.

Eventually, this new reality is just who you are now—the owner of a million-dollar house. It's your new level of normal. Living in a million-dollar house isn't awkward, and it doesn't feel like a stretch. It just is. That is what true manifestation feels like!

When You Don't Do the Work

If you don't do the mindset work but still end up getting what you thought you wanted, it's not going to make you happy. It's because your mindset and your energy didn't change. You're creating results from the same mindset and energetic footprint when you were unhappy, so your creation is designed to keep you unhappy.

It's like people who are constantly getting a new boyfriend or girlfriend and then say, "You know, this relationship isn't working." The new relationship didn't work because they're taking the same energy into every relationship without removing the blocks that are preventing their ideal partner from coming into their life.

The new relationships may look different on the outside, but they all carry the same energetic patterns. These energetic patterns exist in all areas of life, and you will continue to manifest the essence of the same things over and over until you clear your mindset.

If you don't do the mindset work, you'll also continue to chase an elusive dream when it comes to growing your business. You'll keep looking for the next silver bullet, you'll spend hours listening to every marketing and sales guru out there, or you'll spend a ton of money taking a bunch of classes. You're just going to continue to look for all of these outside resources that promise to have the secret...but they don't.

In truth, the secret is inside yourself. You risk the chance of spending thousands of dollars and loads of time on outside resources that don't have the answer that you're looking for. If something really is a great business strategy, you're going to shoot it in the foot because your mindset isn't going to allow you to implement it correctly anyway.

You will self-sabotage it somehow due to the blocks in your subconscious mind. When your mindset isn't clear, you will say that the strategy doesn't work. A lot of times the strategy really would work for your business, but your mindset wouldn't allow it to work.

If this still doesn't make sense to you, one of my favorite sayings is, "Everywhere you go, there you are." What that means is if you don't become the person on the inside that you think you would be by having your desire, then you will be super unhappy once you get what you want. You can be a very successful business owner and be absolutely miserable in your business if you don't remove your mindset blocks and align yourself energetically with your desires.

Once you release the mental barriers keeping you stuck, you can easily move towards what it is that you really want without resistance. That's when the physical thing that you've always wanted is going to manifest faster and easier than you thought it would, and you'll be happy having it because your energy matches your physical creation.

When everything is lined up energetically because you've removed the mental and emotional blocks, things are going to start working for you, and you're going to start feeling better.

Your life in general is just going to start getting easier. Any drama you've had in life or with other people will disappear, and the level of problems you've had will go down.

If you're one of those people who've had boatloads of problems, you're going to actually start seeing the magnitude of those problems lessen, eventually to the point where they will no longer exist.

Albert Einstein said, "The significant problems we have cannot be solved at the same level of thinking with which we created them."

What that means is we are not able to find the solutions to our problems if we don't first clear our mindset. It's because the solution exists on a different energetic frequency. When you do the work, your mindset is clear to receive the answers you need, and the universe helps work your problems out for you.

When there's an energetic mismatch going on inside of you, that's what really creates all the bad feelings and the unhappiness that most people experience. Mindset work seems like the long route to building your dream business, but this is actually the fastest route in disguise.

Most people are not aware that this piece of their business is what they're missing. Once they realize they don't have a mindset free of limiting beliefs and blocks and they're willing to work on themselves, then it makes everything in their business click into place.

Having a clear mindset makes creating everything that you'd like to have in your business easier, whether it's new courses, trainings, or programs. All the information you need to create these projects will just flow through you, and you can quickly create them without much effort.

Clients will start approaching you, and you'll no longer need to chase them. Clients will be after you because everything is in perfect alignment, and they're drawn to your magnetic energy.

When you're in this state of perfect alignment, you're not having to get up every morning nervous or scared that your business is going to fail because it's all just perfectly happening. It's all about you just being in that great mental space that's creating perfect harmony.

If you start working on your mindset, life's going to start getting easier; however, this isn't something you do once and then it's fixed and it's over.

This is a lifelong commitment just like committing to taking care of your health. It must be intentional. You must commit to mindset training if you want to keep moving forward.

If you let go of working on your mindset, you risk allowing all the fear, doubt, worry, overwhelm, and other beliefs back in, and you will be taken away from what it is you want.

Several years ago, a client came to me with many problems in her business. She desperately needed more clients and was brimming with fear she might have to close down her dream and get a job.

She did a lot of inner work and completely transformed herself and her business. She used to joke and say she was the 2.0 version of herself. But she eventually stopped doing the inner work, and her business actually went back to the way it was in the beginning.

It's her mindset controlling the things that she's currently doing in her business, and her self-sabotage is creating the lack of success she so badly wants. If she were to start working on her mindset again, I'm confident she could turn things back around and have the success she deserves.

Most of us know what we should be doing in our businesses to make them successful, but if doubt, fear, worry, and overwhelm creep in, we risk not being able to achieve what we want.

Truthfully as human beings, we're probably not going to get rid of every emotion or belief that's at some level stopping us from becoming who we really are, but we can get to a point where we clear enough blocks to manifest what we want.

Once you get to that point of mental clarity, it's equally as important to maintain it. You don't want to let thoughts creep back in that will sabotage what you've been able to manifest. You stand the risk of losing it all, even if you have already attained it, if you don't continue to do the mindset work.

In my experience, the business owners who do stand up and say, "Yep, I am going to make the commitment to make this part of my daily routine just like taking my vitamins," are forever grateful for the freedom they feel in their life and in their business.

It's because they no longer have the blocks that were once standing in their way. The longer they continue to work on their mindset, the bigger their vision gets, and the more they achieve. This is the path to living a life far beyond your wildest dreams and leaving a legacy for your kids and grandchildren.

What I Wish I'd Known Sooner

Looking back, I wish I'd had this information at my fingertips long before I did, and I wish that I wouldn't have had to piece it all together.

It took a lot of time to figure this all out, and I could have had business success much sooner if a system had already been out there. The good news for you is that there is a system now, and I get to share it with you in the Project Happiness program. You can now implement this information and training in your life and business and not have to wait years like I did to turn your goals and dreams into reality.

In the beginning of my own journey, working on my mindset was very hard because I had so many mindset blocks. When you have a lot of blocks, you're not even aware you have so many of them.

Actually, I laugh about it now, but there was a time when I used to think I didn't have any blocks. I just couldn't believe all these other people had all these problems but not me. That is being in a state of lack of awareness.

Lack of awareness is one way your mindset can play tricks on you and keep you stuck. It makes you think you don't have anything to clear.

When you get started on your own mindset journey, it's okay to not even know where this journey is going to go. You just have to have the desire to be the best version of yourself. You'll be led to wherever you need to clear blocks once you become aware of your thoughts and set the intention that you're ready to do this work.

If you're willing to take the challenge of working on your mindset, know that this process really isn't painful. It can actually be a lot of fun! It's really a deep-dive discovery into who you really are and who you really want to be in this life.

Eventually, you'll be living as your best self, totally mentally and energetically aligned. You'll even start putting your life purpose into action. Then you're on fire for an amazing life where you can do some incredible things, helping tons of people along the way!

Action Steps

1. Get clear. Get clear on what it is that you really, really want in your business and ultimately in your life. Most people use their business as a tool to leverage getting what they want, whether that's time freedom, freedom working from home or working on a laptop computer, or money freedom.

    If you don't know what you really want, write down what you don't like and what you don't want in your current life and business. Then go to the other side of that. If you don't want a lack of clients, for example, how many clients do you want? If you're tired of not making any money in your business, how much money would you like to bring in every month or every year? Your mind cannot create anything that it's not clear about. So, it's your job to get clear.

Once you have some clarity about what direction you're headed, your brain and the universe work as a team to start pulling together the resources that can make what you want a reality. When you're not clear, the vision is too fuzzy, and your brain and the universe don't know what to deliver.

2. Observe your thoughts. Get a notebook and keep it with you. Set a timer, either for every hour or just a few times a day. When the timer goes off, write down what you've been thinking.

   Don't judge the thought, just be an observer, and write down the good, the bad, and the ugly thoughts. After a few days look at what you've written down and start to recognize what you're thinking. Look for patterns. You'll start to see the correlation between your thoughts and the current reality you're living.

3. Join the program. Join the Project Happiness program for a deeper understanding of how this process works, and I'll teach you the exercises you need to permanently remove the programming and blocks that have held you back for so long. Build a mindset that serves your dream business, and most importantly, your ultimate life.

You deserve to have everything that you've ever wanted and more. You are here as a heart-centered entrepreneur, so there's a part of you that already instinctively knows that you are here to change the world and help lots of people.

Be brave enough to step into that challenge fully. The world needs your knowledge and your work.

Remember—you are unique. There's going to be a big void on this planet if you do not step into the space of becoming a successful heart-centered entrepreneur today. Please don't wait.

Let's take the next step towards your success together!

Now's the Time

As a collective, we're moving into a new era of doing business, and because of what's happened in the last handful of years, people have had time to slow down and think about what they really, really want. We've had the ability to step outside of our rat race lifestyle, take a look at things and ask ourselves, "'Is this really how I want to live?', 'Is this really the job or the work that I want to be doing?', Is this the lifestyle that I really want to be living?'"

And an even bigger question I think many people have asked themselves is, "Am I really on the path that I'm supposed to be on?" A lot of people have pondered these thoughts, and as heart-centered entrepreneurs, this is our time to be able to help those people.

The way we help them is through the heart space, by being authentic in who we are, and aligning our businesses with what it is that our clients really, really want from us. We must be able to produce products and services that solve their problems so that they in essence can become their own authentic selves. That is doing business the heart-centered way.

This book was written as the foundation for you to understand this new era of business and to inspire you to look within yourself. As a heart-centered entrepreneur, you are here for a big purpose.

The first step to being able to have your dream business and live in your purpose is to align with who you really are. That way you can do what you were created to do and help lots of people.

But first, you must help yourself. This book is your oxygen mask. Just like being on an airplane, if you don't put your oxygen mask on first, you can't help anybody else. You've got to clear yourself of the barriers that are holding you back from being your authentic, ultimate self.

Once you do, you have now opened the floodgates to everything you've ever wanted, with even more to come your way. It's simply a matter of dedicating just a few minutes a day to working on your mindset.